Wonders of the World
Grand Canyon

Michelle Lomberg

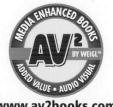

www.av2books.com

AV² provides enriched content that supplements and complements this book. Weigl's AV² books strive to create inspired learning and engage young minds in a total learning experience.

Your AV² Media Enhanced books come alive with...

Audio
Listen to sections of the book read aloud.

Key Words
Study vocabulary, and complete a matching word activity.

Video
Watch informative video clips.

Quizzes
Test your knowledge.

Embedded Weblinks
Gain additional information for research.

Slide Show
View images and captions, and prepare a presentation.

Try This!
Complete activities and hands-on experiments.

... and much, much more!

Go to **www.av2books.com**, and enter this book's unique code.

BOOK CODE

F 6 2 9 1 1 0

AV² **by Weigl** brings you media enhanced books that support active learning.

Published by AV² by Weigl
350 5th Avenue, 59th Floor
New York, NY 10118
Website: www.av2books.com   www.weigl.com

Library of Congress Cataloging-in-Publication Data

Lomberg, Michelle.
 Grand Canyon : wonders of the world / Michelle Lomberg.
   p. cm.
 Includes index.
 Includes links to multimedia content.
 ISBN 978-1-61913-524-6 (hard cover : alk. paper) -- ISBN 978-1-61913-437-9 (soft cover : alk. paper) -- ISBN 978-1-61913-614-4 (ebook)
 1. Grand Canyon (Ariz.) -- Juvenile literature. I. Title.
 F788.L794 2013
 979.1'32--dc23
                                    2012010886

062012
WEP170512

Project Coordinator Heather Kissock
Design Mandy Christiansen

Contents

A Canyon of Wonders

Imagine a hole in the ground as large as the state of Delaware. The Grand Canyon is that size. It is the largest canyon in the United States. The canyon and surrounding area make up Grand Canyon National Park.

The Grand Canyon was created by the moving waters of the Colorado River. It was formed by a process called **erosion**, over a period of about 6 million years. Humans began to live in and around the canyon more than 4,000 years ago.

Today, visitors to the Grand Canyon can learn about the canyon's vibrant Native-American culture. They can observe the many different types of local plants and animals in the area.

Rocks at the bottom of the Grand Canyon are nearly 2 billion years old. These are some of the oldest rocks on Earth.

Desert bighorn sheep roam the canyon's cliffs.

Grand Canyon Facts

- The Grand Canyon is about 280 miles (450 kilometers) long.
- At its widest point, the Grand Canyon is 18 miles (29 km) wide. The canyon's **average** width is 10 miles (16 km).
- The average depth of the Grand Canyon is 1 mile (1.6 km).
- The Glen Canyon Dam controls the flow of the Colorado River through the Grand Canyon.
- Grand Canyon National Park was established in 1919.
- The Grand Canyon is one of the **Seven Natural Wonders of the World**.

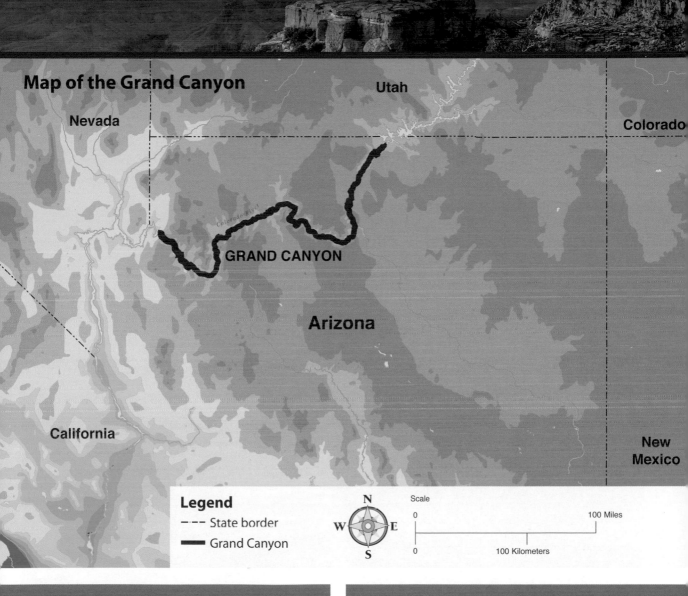

Map of the Grand Canyon

Nevada

Utah

Colorado

Colorado River

GRAND CANYON

Arizona

California

New
Mexico

Legend

-·-·- State border

—— Grand Canyon

N
W · E
S

Scale

0   100 Miles

0   100 Kilometers

On clear days, the Colorado River reflects the sky above.

Boaters explore the inner canyon and camp along the river's shores and beaches.

Where in the World?

Grand Canyon National Park is located in northwestern Arizona. The Colorado River flows through the canyon. The river is 1,450 miles (2,333 km) long. Beginning in Colorado at Rocky Mountain National Park, the river flows all the way down to the Gulf of California in Mexico.

The weather in the Grand Canyon is extreme. Summer temperatures can reach up to 105° Fahrenheit (41°Celsius) at the bottom of the canyon. The canyon's South Rim can vary in temperature between 50°F (10°C) and 80°F (27°C). The North Rim can be even cooler. Winter brings snow and ice to the Grand Canyon's rims. The weather in spring and fall is unpredictable.

The elevation of the Grand Canyon ranges from about 2,000 feet (610 m) to more than 8,000 feet (2,440 m). These differences in elevation contribute to a variety of weather conditions. Many roads and trails may be closed during winter.

The arid, rocky landscape of the Grand Canyon is typical of the Southwest region of the United States.

Q: What are the names of the **geographical** regions of the United States? Locate them on the map.

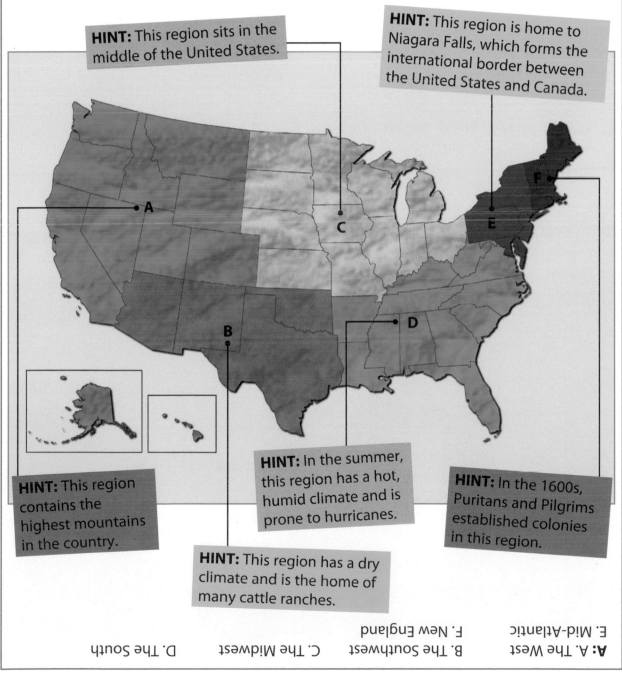

HINT: This region sits in the middle of the United States.

HINT: This region is home to Niagara Falls, which forms the international border between the United States and Canada.

HINT: This region contains the highest mountains in the country.

HINT: In the summer, this region has a hot, humid climate and is prone to hurricanes.

HINT: In the 1600s, Puritans and Pilgrims established colonies in this region.

HINT: This region has a dry climate and is the home of many cattle ranches.

A: A. The West   B. The Southwest   C. The Midwest   D. The South   E. Mid-Atlantic   F. New England

A Trip Back in Time

The different layers of rocks found in the Grand Canyon provide a fascinating record of the region's **geological** history. Each layer of rock is from a different time period. The layers are visible because they are made up of different substances and colors.

The layers of rocks tell scientists that the Grand Canyon's environment was once very different. In the past, shallow seas advanced and retreated, covering the area several times.

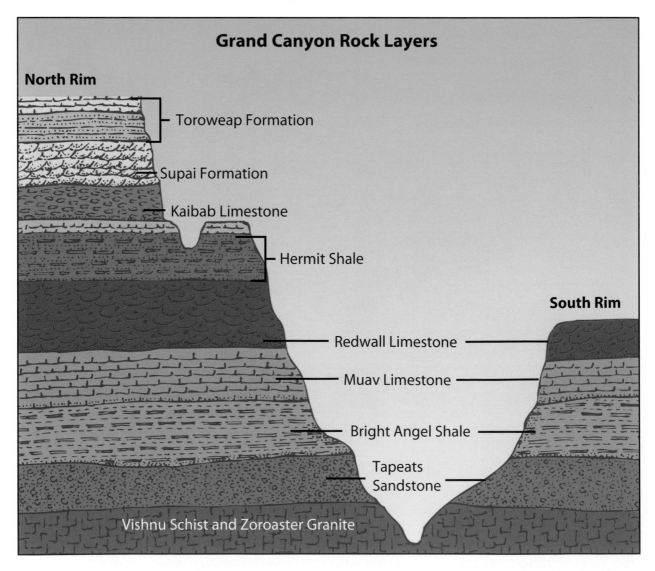

Grand Canyon Rock Layers

North Rim
- Toroweap Formation
- Supai Formation
- Kaibab Limestone
- Hermit Shale

South Rim
- Redwall Limestone
- Muav Limestone
- Bright Angel Shale
- Tapeats Sandstone

Vishnu Schist and Zoroaster Granite

Rock Origins

All of the rocks found on Earth are identified according to how they are formed. The three main rock categories are igneous, sedimentary, and metamorphic. All three types can be found in the Grand Canyon.

Fire Rocks

Beneath Earth's **crust** is a layer of **molten** rock called magma. When magma reaches Earth's surface and cools, it becomes igneous rock. Igneous means "made in fire."

The rock at the eastern end of the canyon, called Cardenas Basalt, is igneous rock. It was formed by volcanoes millions of years ago.

Settled Rocks

Sedimentary rocks consist of tiny rock particles called sediment. These particles are carried by water, ice, or wind until they settle and form a layer. Over millions of years, this layer hardens into rock. The limestone and sandstone layers of the Grand Canyon are sedimentary rocks.

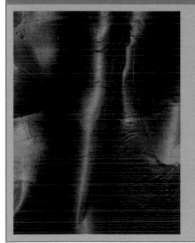

Changed Rocks

Metamorphic rocks are formed when existing rocks are exposed to extreme heat and pressure. Metamorphic means "changed." The Vishnu Schist layer, found at the bottom of the Grand Canyon, is metamorphic rock. The Vishnu Schist was formed 2 billion years ago. Tremendous pressure twisted layers of sedimentary rock into a huge mountain range.

Geology at Work

The Grand Canyon was created by two geological processes. These processes are called weathering and erosion.

Weathering is the process that breaks large rocks into smaller rocks and rock particles. Weathering cracks, breaks, or wears away at rocks. Plants and tree roots can break rocks apart. Freezing and thawing can also crack rocks. Acid rain and tiny plants, called lichens, can eat away at rocks.

Erosion carries away the small pieces of rock created by weathering in wind, water, or ice. Rock particles act like sandpaper, wearing away large rocks over time. In the Grand Canyon, erosion is caused by the Colorado River and by wind and rain. The Grand Canyon's towers, folds, and valleys were all created by erosion.

The rock layers in the Grand Canyon walls responded differently to weathering and erosion. Some rocks formed cliffs, others formed slopes, and some eroded more quickly than others.

The Rock Cycle

Earth relies on natural systems to recycle matter and energy. The rock cycle is one of many natural recycling programs. This cycle takes millions of years to complete.

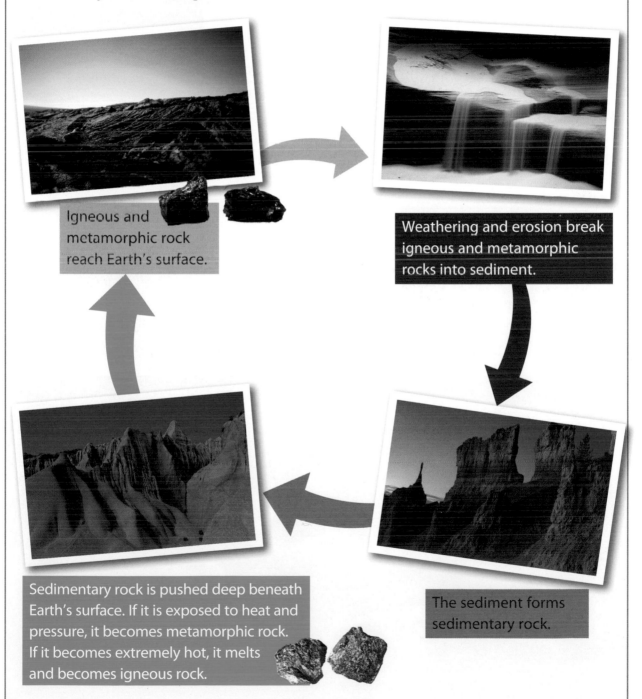

Igneous and metamorphic rock reach Earth's surface.

Weathering and erosion break igneous and metamorphic rocks into sediment.

Sedimentary rock is pushed deep beneath Earth's surface. If it is exposed to heat and pressure, it becomes metamorphic rock. If it becomes extremely hot, it melts and becomes igneous rock.

The sediment forms sedimentary rock.

Life in the Canyon

Naturalists divide the Grand Canyon into four main areas. They are the North Rim, the South Rim, the inner canyon, and the inner **gorge**. Each area has its own types of animal and plant life.

At 8,200 feet (2,500 m) above sea level, the North Rim is the highest and coolest part of the canyon. The South Rim is lower and slightly warmer. The dense trees and bushes of the rims provide homes for animals such as mule deer and coyotes. The rare Kaibab squirrel can only be found in the ponderosa pines on the North Rim.

The inner canyon includes the area between the bottom of the canyon and the rims. Flowering plants and cacti thrive in the inner canyon. Bighorn sheep graze among the rocks. Reptiles bask on the sun-warmed stones.

Beavertail and other cactus bloom in the spring.

The plants and animals of the inner gorge live along the banks of the Colorado River. Columbine and monkey flowers bloom among the cottonwood trees. Ducks and great blue herons float on the river. Rainbow trout and other fish swim in the cool waters.

Although bighorn sheep are protected in the Grand Canyon, little is known about their distribution or population in the park.

Life Zones

Elevation describes how high the land is above sea level. Different types of plants, or vegetation, grow at different elevations. Some scientists divide the Grand Canyon into life zones based on elevation. In the Grand Canyon, the Lower Sonoran Zone occupies the lowest elevation. The Upper Sonoran Zone falls in the middle, and the Transition Zone is at the highest elevation.

Life Zones of the Grand Canyon		
Lower Sonoran Zone	**Upper Sonoran Zone**	**Transition Zone**
Height Above Sea Level 0–3,500 feet (0–1,067 m)	3,500–7,000 feet (1,067–2,134 m)	7,000–8,250 feet (2,134–2,515 m)
Area of Canyon Inner Gorge	Inner Canyon	North and South Rims
Vegetation Desert Plants, Sparse Vegetation	Juniper, Piñon Pine, Dry Grassland	Ponderosa Pine Forests

Early Explorers

In 1540, García López de Cárdenas, a soldier from Spain, became the first European to visit the Grand Canyon. In the mid-1800s, explorers traveled down the Colorado River to learn more about what they called the "big canyon." The United States government sent an engineer named Joseph Ives to map the area in 1857. Twelve years later, John Wesley Powell led an **expedition** through the Colorado River.

John Wesley Powell spent 30 years studying the Native Peoples of the American West.

Along with 10 men and four boats, John Wesley Powell explored about 1,000 miles (1,600 km) of the Grand Canyon. Powell lost many of his boats and provisions in the rough water. Half of his exhausted men left the expedition. Some of them died.

John Wesley Powell (1834–1902)

As a young boy, John Wesley Powell had a keen interest in nature and geology. He loved to collect shells and rocks near his home in Mount Morris, New York. Powell became a teacher when he grew up. Later, he became a professor of geology. In 1869, Powell arranged an expedition of the Colorado River. Powell's group was the first to paddle down the Colorado River. It took the crew 14 weeks to travel through the canyon. Powell was the first person to call the area the Grand Canyon.

Facts of Life

Born: March 24, 1834

Hometown: Mount Morris, New York

Occupation: Soldier, geologist, teacher, professor, and explorer

Died: September 23, 1902

The Big Picture

River canyons exist in many places around the world. They were created over millions of years as water and wind wore away layers of rock, leaving amazing landscapes. This map shows some of the deepest and largest canyons in the world.

PACIFIC OCEAN

NORTH AMERICA

ATLANTIC OCEAN

Mexico
Copper Canyon
6,136 feet (1,870 m) deep

SOUTH AMERICA

Peru
Colca Canyon
10,433 feet (3,180 m) deep

SOUTHERN OCEAN

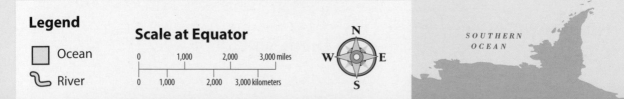

Legend

☐ Ocean

〜 River

Scale at Equator

0   1,000   2,000   3,000 miles

0   1,000   2,000   3,000 kilometers

N
W · E
S

Montenegro
Tara River Canyon
4,265 feet (1,300 m) deep

China
Canyons of Wulingyuan
Scenic Area
Includes 32 canyons, each
more than 6,560 feet
(2,000 m) long

ASIA

EUROPE

PACIFIC
OCEAN

AFRICA

EQUATOR

INDIAN
OCEAN

AUSTRALIA

Namibia
Fish River Canyon
1,800 feet (549 m) deep

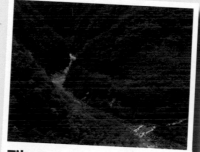

Tibet
Great Canyon of Yarlung
Tsangpo River
17,657 feet (5,382 m) deep

SOUTHERN
OCEAN

ANTARCTICA

People of the Canyon

Humans have lived in and around the Grand Canyon for thousands of years—long before the first Europeans arrived. **Hunter-gatherers** passed through the area as early as 11,000 BC. Around 2,000 BC, another group of people occupied the area. They left behind animal figures made out of willow twigs.

By AD 500, the Anasazi had settled in the canyon area. The Anasazi left the area in the 13th century. They were likely forced to leave because of drought. In the 1300s, the Cerbat and the Southern Paiute peoples settled in the canyon.

Today, Native Americans still live in the Grand Canyon area. The Hualapai and the Havasupai live in the western part of the canyon. They are descendants of the Cerbat. The Navajo live around the eastern end of the canyon.

Some believe that the Hopi are descendants of the Anasazi. The Hopi live east of the Grand Canyon.

Puzzler

The earliest Anasazi are referred to as Basket Makers. Using fibers from plants that grow in the Grand Canyon, the Anasazi made baskets in a variety of sizes, shapes, textures, and patterns.

Q: Why did the Anasazi find baskets useful?

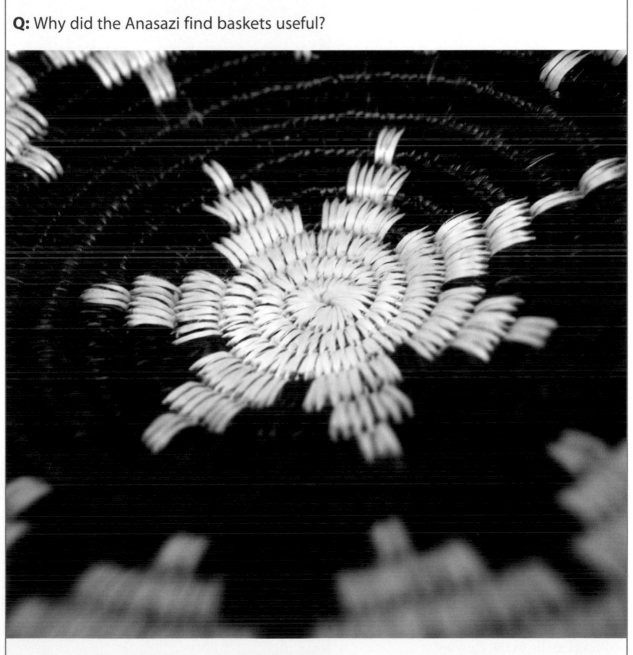

A: Anasazi baskets were light to carry. They were made from local materials that were easy to find. They were also well-suited to the arid climate of the inner canyon.

Timeline

1.25 billion years ago

A sea floods the area where the Grand Canyon is located today, depositing sediment that will harden into rock.

1.25–1 billion years ago

Volcanoes erupt in the area. The lava will become igneous rock.

1 billion–250 million years ago

Shallow seas advance and retreat, creating layers of sedimentary rock.

248 million years ago

Dinosaurs and mammals begin to evolve.

66 million years ago

A mass extinction kills the dinosaurs.

20 million years ago

The Colorado River begins to carve the eastern end of the Grand Canyon.

5 million years ago

The Colorado River changes course, now running the length of the Grand Canyon.

120,000 years ago

The first modern humans evolve.

11,000 BC

Hunter-gatherers pass through the area.

1000 BC–2000 BC

Early peoples pass through the canyon, leaving cave drawings.

500 BC–AD 1200

The Anasazi settle in the canyon.

AD 1300

The Cerbat and the Southern Paiute cultures settle in the canyon.

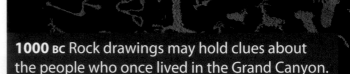

1000 BC Rock drawings may hold clues about the people who once lived in the Grand Canyon.

Present The Colorado River is 1,450 miles (2,333 km) long, from the state of Colorado to the Gulf of California. The river runs 277 miles (446 km) through the Grand Canyon.

1910s Hopi women continue to weave baskets in the same ways as their ancestors.

Present Today, most Southern Paiute live in southern Utah and northern Arizona, just north of the Grand Canyon.

1900s Theodore Roosevelt, the 26th US president, creates five national parks.

ARIZONA

Grand Canyon

Santa Fe is the only railroad entering this National Park

Santa Fe

1930s Train trips to the canyon become popular.

Present Lake Powell, which is located behind the Glen Canyon Dam, is 560 feet (171 m) deep and about 186 miles (299 km) long when full.

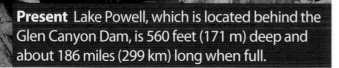

2007 The skywalk opens, giving visitors another way to experience the canyon.

Present Hundreds of tourists fly over the canyon each day.

1860s
The Navajo settle in the area.

1869
John Wesley Powell explores the Grand Canyon.

1893
The Grand Canyon Forest Preserve is created.

1901
The first train service brings tourists to the canyon.

1906
President Theodore Roosevelt creates the Grand Canyon Game Reserve.

1919
Grand Canyon National Park is created.

1956
The number of visitors to Grand Canyon National Park reaches 1 million.

1964
The Glen Canyon Dam across the Colorado River is completed.

1979
The Grand Canyon becomes a **World Heritage Site**.

2000
Close to 5 million people visit the Grand Canyon.

2007
The Grand Canyon Skywalk, a glass walkway, opens to the public.

2011
More than 400,000 tourists view the Grand Canyon from the air.

Too Many Tourists, Too Much Pollution

Nearly 5 million people visit Grand Canyon National Park every year. The Grand Canyon is slowly being worn down by tourist use. It needs many expensive improvements to its infrastructure. Campgrounds, sewers, and roads all need to be improved.

Some visitors leave garbage behind. Water bottles became such a problem that in 2012 the park banned the sale of water in disposable containers. Most visitors travel in their vehicles, which causes air pollution. Tourist flights over the canyon have added both visual and noise pollution. Coal-fired power plants and major cities, as well as the steady flow of vehicles, are the main causes of air pollution in the region. A hazy smog often prevents tourists from enjoying the beautiful scenery of the Grand Canyon.

In addition, exploratory drilling for uranium has caused great environmental concern. Scientists are concerned about the long-term effect of uranium mines and the impact mining could have on water supplies in the region.

Summer winds carry pollutants to the Grand Canyon from urban and industrial areas in southern California, Arizona, and New Mexico.

Government officials are trying to protect the Grand Canyon. They want to improve public transportation so that fewer people will drive to the canyon and from point to point within the canyon. Park officials are working with the Federal Aviation Administration to regulate flights over the canyon. They are also working with the United States Geological Society to address the environmental problems related to mining.

Should the government limit the number of tourists to the Grand Canyon?

Yes	No
The Grand Canyon National Park is too crowded. Limiting the number of tourists will decrease crowds and automobile traffic.	People already have to plan months in advance to visit the canyon. Limiting access will make visiting the park even more difficult.
The Grand Canyon is being damaged by overuse, litter, and pollution. It must be protected.	If people use public transportation, stay on the trails, and pick up their litter, the canyon will not be damaged.
Human traffic scares away the wildlife.	Everyone should have the opportunity to see the Grand Canyon's unique plants and animals.

Natural Attractions

There are many ways to experience the wonders of the Grand Canyon, whether for a few hours or a few days. For a spectacular view of the canyon, visit the Yavapai Observation Station at Yavapai Point. The station features three-dimensional models and exhibits on the region's history and geology.

Hiking is a popular way to experience the beauty of the Grand Canyon.

Try a short hike on the Bright Angel Trail. The path is well-maintained and offers shade, water, and rest areas along the way.

For a hearty meal, visit the historic Phantom Ranch. Visitors can travel to the ranch on foot or by mule.

Take a trip down the Colorado River. It can take up to 18 days to row the entire length of the Grand Canyon. Rafters ride the rapids by day and camp along the banks of the Colorado River at night.

You Can Help

There are several ways to help preserve the Grand Canyon. When visiting the park, visitors must obey the following rules.

Leave no trace of your visit. This means taking out what you bring with you. Never litter.

Do not light fires.

Walk only on the main trails.

Never feed the animals.

Avoid using a vehicle if you can. Trains and buses travel to the canyon from nearby towns.

Be Prepared

Some planning will help make any trip safe and enjoyable. When hiking the Grand Canyon, it is important to have some basic equipment with you.

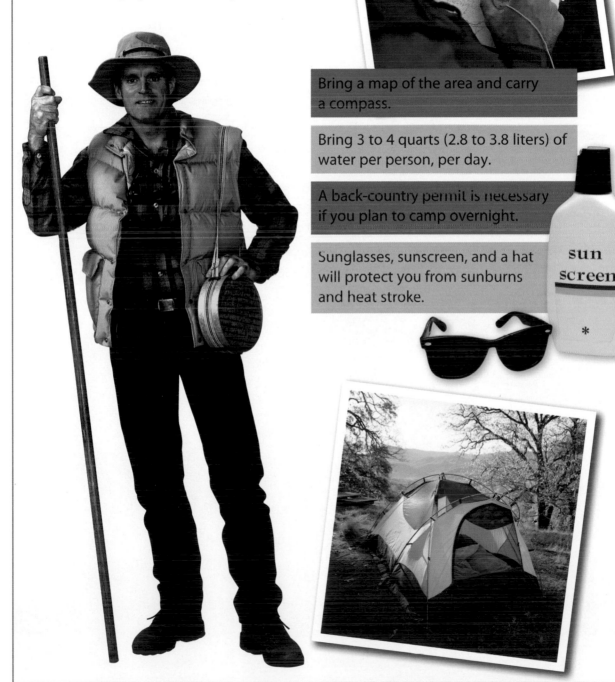

Bring a map of the area and carry a compass.

Bring 3 to 4 quarts (2.8 to 3.8 liters) of water per person, per day.

A back-country permit is necessary if you plan to camp overnight.

Sunglasses, sunscreen, and a hat will protect you from sunburns and heat stroke.

sun screen

*

Grand Artistic Heritage

The Grand Canyon is rich in art and culture. Its heritage dates back thousands of years. Cave drawings, twig figures, baskets, and pottery record the artistry of early canyon dwellers.

The Grand Canyon continues to inspire artists today. Artists at several of the area's reservations make beautiful pottery, dolls, beadwork, and jewelry. Painters and photographers try to capture the magic of the canyon in their work.

Navajo pottery is sold around the world.

Navajo sandpainting began as a spiritual healing system. The figures represent characters in Navajo stories.

The Navajo are well known for their silver and turquoise jewelry.

Canyon Mythology

The Hopi believe that their ancestors traveled to Earth's surface from below the ground. In Hopi **mythology**, the Grand Canyon represents *Sipapu*. Sipapu is the hole through which their ancestors emerged. It is also the place where spirits of the dead go to rest.

Hopi kachina dancers dress to represent ancestral spirits or objects in nature such as the Sun, the stars, or the wind. The dances help teach young people Hopi traditions and beliefs.

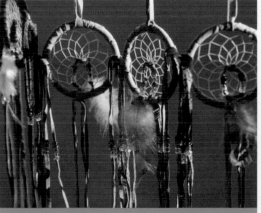

The Navajo people make dreamcatchers to hang above their beds. According to legend, the dreamcatcher will catch the bad dreams and let the good dreams through to those who sleep.

Hopi ceremonial dances and rituals are performed to drive away evil forces and to keep the world in harmony and balance.

What Have You Learned?

True or False?

Decide whether the following statements are true or false.
If the statement is false, make it true.

1. The Colorado River carved the Grand Canyon in fewer than 1,000 years.

2. Winter weather at the Grand Canyon includes snow and ice.

3. Native Americans live in the Grand Canyon.

4. In summer, the bottom of the Grand Canyon is cool and humid.

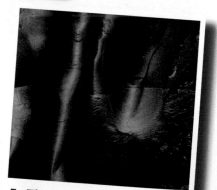

5. The Vishnu Schist rock layer is about 2 billion years old.

ANSWERS

1. False. It took the Colorado River almost 6 million years to carve out the Grand Canyon.
2. True
3. True
4. False. In summer, the bottom of the Grand Canyon is hot.
5. True

Short Answer

Answer the following questions using information from the book.

1. What is the average depth of the Grand Canyon?

2. In which area of the Grand Canyon is the Kaibab squirrel found?

3. What controls the flow of the Colorado River through the Grand Canyon?

4. Who was the first European to reach the Grand Canyon?

5. In what year was Grand Canyon National Park created?

Multiple Choice

Choose the best answer for the following questions.

1. In which state is Grand Canyon National Park located?
   a. Colorado
   b. Utah
   c. Arizona
   d. Nevada

2. In which region of the U.S. is Grand Canyon National Park located?
   a. South
   b. Southwest
   c. Midwest
   d. West

3. In what year did John Wesley Powell lead his expedition down the Colorado River?
   a. 1869
   b. 1858
   c. 1919
   d. 1901

4. Which group settled in the Grand Canyon around 500 BC?
   a. the Cerbat
   b. the Hopi
   c. the Havasupai
   d. the Anasazi

Activity

Water Erosion

Water erosion played a big role in the formation of the Grand Canyon. Water, either dripping or flowing over millions of years, can wear away even the strongest, densest kinds of rock. Try this experiment to see how sand can be eroded by water.

Materials

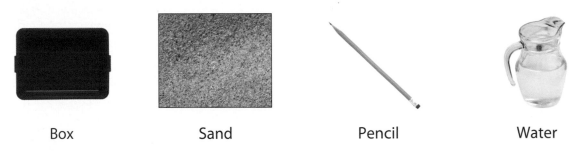

Box   Sand   Pencil   Water

Instructions

1 Fill the box with sand, about 1 inch (2.5 cm) deep, and then elevate one end of the box 15° to 20°.

2 Make a wedge on one corner of the box.

3 Use the pencil to make a series of horizontal ridges in the sand. The ridges should be about .5 inches (1.25 cm) deep and 1 inch (2.5 cm) apart.

4 Sprinkle or slowly pour water into the box. Let the water settle and stand for about 15 minutes.

5 Measure the depth and width of the gullies and of the ridges.

Results

As you dripped the water into the box, you probably saw it settle in between the ridges and create deeper gullies between the ridges. This is how canyons are created. Water cuts deep channels through the stone.

Key Words

average: a calculated number found by adding two or more numbers together, then dividing by the sum of the number of items added

crust: outermost hard layer of Earth

erosion: gradual wearing away of rock

expedition: voyage that has a particular purpose

geographical: relating to the study of Earth's surface

geological: relating to the study of Earth's rocks and minerals

gorge: steep-sided valley

hunter-gatherers: people who survive by hunting animals and gathering plants for their food

molten: made liquid by heat

mythology: traditional stories that explain ancient times or natural events

Seven Natural Wonders of the World: the Great Barrier Reef, Australia; the Grand Canyon, United States; the harbor of Rio de Janeiro, Brazil; Mount Everest, Nepal; the northern lights; Paricutin volcano, Mexico; Victoria Falls, Zimbabwe

World Heritage Site: a place that is of natural or cultural importance to the entire world

Index

Log on to www.av2books.com

AV² by Weigl brings you media enhanced books that support active learning. Go to www.av2books.com, and enter the special code found on page 2 of this book. You will gain access to enriched and enhanced content that supplements and complements this book. Content includes video, audio, weblinks, quizzes, a slide show, and activities.

Audio
Listen to sections of the book read aloud.

Video
Watch informative video clips.

Embedded Weblinks
Gain additional information for research.

Try This!
Complete activities and hands-on experiments.

WHAT'S ONLINE?

Try This!	Embedded Weblinks	Video	EXTRA FEATURES
Map where the Grand Canyon is and the features that surround it. Write a biography of an explorer who traveled the Grand Canyon region. Locate major canyons around the world. Complete a timeline that outlines the history of the Grand Canyon. Test your knowledge of the Grand Canyon.	Learn more about the Grand Canyon. Play games related to the Grand Canyon. Find out more about early explorers of the Grand Canyon.	Take a flight over the Grand Canyon. Watch this video to learn more about the issues facing the Grand Canyon.	**Audio** Listen to sections of the book read aloud. **Key Words** Study vocabulary, and complete a matching word activity. **Slide Show** View images and captions, and prepare a presentation. **Quizzes** Test your knowledge.

AV² was built to bridge the gap between print and digital. We encourage you to tell us what you like and what you want to see in the future.

Sign up to be an AV² Ambassador at www.av2books.com/ambassador.